Weekly Reader Books presents

What to do when your mom or dad says . . .
"TAKE CARE OF YOUR CLOTHES!"

By

JOY WILT BERRY

Living Skills Press
Fallbrook, California

Distributed by:

Celestial Arts
231 Adrian Road
Millbrae, CA 94030

CREDITS

Producer
  Ron Berry

Editor
  Orly Kelly

Weekly Reader Books edition published by
arrangement with Living Skills Press.

Dear Parents:

"TAKE CARE OF YOUR CLOTHES!" You've probably said that more than once to your child and received a less than enthusiastic response. Has it ever occurred to you that your child's resistance to your request may come from not knowing **how** to do what you have asked? The assumption that a child will automatically know how to fulfill a request is often the cause of much parent-child conflict.

If you expect your children to do something they are not equipped to do, it is most likely that they will become overwhelmed and anxious while you become frustrated. Both reactions are prime conditions for an argument!

Why not avoid these kinds of encounters? Who needs them? Much of the negative "back and forth" which goes on between you and your child could be avoided if both of you approach your expectations intelligently.

Fulfilling **any** expectation always begins with knowing how. Skills are required to do any task, no matter what the task may be. These skills must be learned **before** the task can be accomplished. This is a fact of life!

All too often parents have left their children to discover these skills on their own through trial and error over a very long period of time. But why should this be so? You wouldn't give your child a complicated book in the beginning and say, "Teach yourself to read!"

My suspicion is that most parents take certain skills so much for granted, they forget that these skills must be taught.

Does this apply to you? If it does, **relax** because **"TAKE CARE OF YOUR CLOTHES!"** not only helps children, it helps parents survive as well.

If you will take the time to go through this book with your child, both of you will learn some valuable skills — skills that will really pay off in the long run.

Some children will be able to read the book and assimilate all of the information themselves; however, in most cases you'll get better, longer lasting results if you use the "show me how, then let me do it" method. Here's how it works:

Using this book as a guideline ...

1. Demonstrate how the task should be done by doing it yourself while your child watches.

2. Do the task together or encourage your child to do the task while you watch. (Avoid criticizing his or her efforts, and praise anything done correctly while you are watching.)

3. Let your child do the task alone.

4. Praise your child's work and express appreciation for what he or she has done.

If you'll take a little bit of time to teach your children the skills they need to fulfill your requests, you'll save yourself a lot of energy in the long haul.

So don't just sit there – do it, and have fun while you're at it. Who knows, doing these nitty-gritty things with your child may give you some of the greatest experiences you'll ever have together, and surely some of the most rewarding.

Sincerely,

Joy Wilt Berry

Has your mother or father ever told you to ...

TAKE CARE OF YOUR CLOTHES!

When your parents ask you to take care of your clothes, do you ever wonder ...

If any of this sounds familiar to you, you're going to **love** this book!

Because this book is going to tell you exactly what to do to take care of your clothes.

GETTING YOUR CLOTHES

There are four ways to get clothes:

1. You can buy new clothes from a store.

2. You can buy used clothes from a
   secondhand store.

3. You can trade some of your used clothing
   for someone else's used clothing.

4. You can get used clothes from someone who has outgrown them.

No matter where you get your clothes, you need to make sure that they —

1. are comfortable to wear;

2. are appropriate for where you are going to wear them (for example, make sure your school clothes meet your school's requirements);

3. fit well;

4. are easy to put on and take off;

5. are easy to take care of;

6. are sturdy;

7. make you look good; and

8. make you feel good about yourself when you wear them.

Get rid of worn or outgrown clothes before you put any new ones away so you won't have to dig through a pile of old clothes to get to the new ones.

Label your clothes so that if they're ever misplaced they can be returned to you.

If you are like many children, your clothes will need to be washed after you've worn them once. If your family is like many others, your laundry gets washed only once a week. If these things are true, you will need several different outfits.

In addition, you will probably need to get clothes for yourself twice a year. This is because —

– you are growing;

– the seasons change and you need both warm and cool clothing; and

– if you're like many children, you wear your clothes out in six months.

The two charts on the following pages will give you an idea of what clothes you will most likely need for a six-month period.

Clothing for a Six-Month Period - Girls

AMOUNT	ITEM
2	Nighties or pajamas
1	Bathrobe
1	Slippers
7	Panties
1	Slip
7*	Pairs of socks
2**	Pairs of shoes
1	Boots
5	Play / school outfits
2	Dress-up outfits
1	Warm coat
1	Raincoat
1	Lightweight jacket
1	Nice sweater
1	Set of snow clothes (if you live where winters are cold)
1-2	Bathing suits
1-2	Purses

* 5 for every day, 2 for dress-up
** 1 for play, the other for dress-up

Clothing for a Six-Month Period - Boys

AMOUNT	ITEM
2	Pajamas
1	Bathrobe
1	Slippers
7	Underwear
7*	Pairs of socks
2**	Pairs of shoes
1	Boots
5-7	Shirts
5	Sturdy play / school pants
2	Dress-up outfits
1	Warm coat
1	Raincoat
1	Lightweight jacket or sweatshirt
1	Set of snow clothes (if you live where winters are cold)
1-2	Bathing suits
1	Wallet

* 5 for every day, 2 for dress-up
** 1 for play, the other for dress-up

WASHING YOUR CLOTHES

Always put your dirty clothes in a clothes hamper (or whatever the dirty clothes are kept in) so that they will eventually get washed.

If your parents are too busy to wash your clothes as often as you need them washed, learn to wash, dry and fold your own clothes. If you have an automatic washing machine and/or dryer in your home, learn to use them properly.

THIS OUGHT TO BE GOOD!

If you don't have a washing machine, or if you have only a few things that need washing, you can wash your clothes in a sink and hang them out to dry. To do this, follow these steps:

1. Vigorously slosh the garment around in warm soapy water for several minutes or until it looks as if the dirt has been removed.

2. Wring as much of the soapy water as possible out of the garment by squeezing and twisting it.

3. Slosh the garment around in clear water for several minutes or until the soap has been removed.

4. Wring as much of the water as possible out of the garment.

5. Using fresh water, repeat steps 3 and 4.

6. Hang the garment up to dry (on a clothesline, in a shower or bathtub, or on a clothes drying rack).

THIS ISN'T FUNNY.

Whether you wash your clothes by machine or in a sink, here are a few tips on how to do a good job:

Don't wash dark and bright-colored clothes with white and light-colored clothes because colors may run and darken the white or light-colored clothes.

Dark and bright-colored clothes should be washed in cold or lukewarm water.

White and light-colored clothes should be washed in warm or hot water.

Be sure that you know exactly what to do before you use a —
– stain remover
– detergent
– bleach
– fabric softener.

Too much of any one of these things can ruin your clothes. To make sure you do not misuse any of these products, carefully read the instructions on each container or get an adult to show you what to do.

If your clothes have very dirty spots on them, rub a stain remover, liquid detergent, or dry detergent mixed with water on the spot, let it stand for a few minutes, then add it to the wash.

* If you hang your clothes up to dry, avoid using metal clips or hangers as they will rust your clothes.

* If you dry your clothes in a dryer, don't run the machine too hot or too long because it could ruin your clothes.

* Hang or fold your clothes immediately after they have been dried so they don't get wrinkled.

HANGING YOUR CLOTHES

To hang your clothes properly, do these things:

Blouses, skirts, jackets and dresses should hang on a hanger the same way they hang on your shoulders, with the top button buttoned or the zipper zipped.

23

Skirts should hang on skirt hangers or they can be pinned on wire hangers with safety pins.

Pants should be smoothed out with a crease running down the middle of each leg, then hung by the cuffs with an equal amount of the pants hanging on each side of the hanger.

THE OPPOSITE OF PANTS!

CUTE!

FOLDING YOUR CLOTHES

To fold a T-shirt, knit top or sweater —

1. Spread it out, front down;

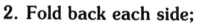

2. Fold back each side;

3. Fold the arms down;

4. Fold up the bottom.

Underwear should be smoothed out and folded in half. Shorts can be folded the same way.

Socks should be matched and then folded in thirds. Don't pull the top down over the folded socks because that stretches the top of the socks and they won't stay up when you wear them.

Belts should be rolled or hung.

ROTATING YOUR CLOTHES

To make sure that you do not wear some of your clothes more than others —

– Put your clean clothes on the **bottom** of the stacks in your cupboards and drawers.

- Always use the clothes off the **top** of each
  stack of clean clothes.

To rotate the clothes in your closet, put the clean clothes in back of the clothes that are hanging.

Always use the clothes from the front of the clothes that are hanging.

If you rotate your clothes, you will not wear some out before others and you will not end up wearing the same thing over and over again.

CLEANING YOUR SHOES

If you have washable tennis shoes —

– Wash them as often as they need it (refer to the instructions on page 18).

– Set them aside to dry. Do not dry tennis shoes in an automatic clothes dryer because the heat will ruin the rubber and shrink the shoes.

If you have shoes that can't be polished (like suede shoes) —

– Knock any loose dirt off the shoes by banging them together several times.

- Brush the remainder of the dirt off the shoes with a clean stiff brush.

If you have shoes that can be polished, follow these steps:

1. Clean the dirt off the shoes with a slightly damp cloth.

2. Following the directions on the shoe polish container, put polish on the shoes.

3. Let the polish dry.

4. Buff each shoe with a soft clean cloth until it shines.

Don't forget to wash your shoelaces whenever they need it, and replace them when they start to look worn or are about to break.

MENDING YOUR CLOTHES

Have a special place in your room or in another room in your house to put clothes that need mending, and be sure to tell the person who mends your clothes about repairs you need done.

If no one else mends your clothes for you, you can do it yourself. The next few pages will show you how.

SEW SEW

SO WHAT?

TO SEW ON A BUTTON

You will need —

1. the button which has come off; or

2. a button about the same size as the missing one, which matches the other buttons if there are any;

3. thread to match your button or your fabric;

4. a needle which will fit through the holes in your button.

STEPS:

1. Cut a length of thread as long as your arm.

2. Thread the needle, join the two ends of thread, and tie a knot.

3. Place the button in the spot where you want it sewn, and hold it in place with your thumb and forefinger.

4. Pass the needle through from the back of the fabric and through one of the holes in the button. Pull gently until the knot in your thread catches at the back of the button.

5. Now pass the needle through a hole in the top of the button. Continue to hold the button in place, being careful not to cover the button with your finger when the needle comes through from the back — OUCH!!

6. Continue to pass the needle back and forth through the buttonholes until the button feels securely fastened.

7. Cut the thread from the needle on the underside of the button and tie a knot very close to the fabric.

TO REPAIR A SEAM

You will need —

1. a needle;

2. thread to match the color of the clothing being repaired;

3. a ruler;

4. chalk or a pencil;

5. an iron;

6. an ironing board.

STEPS:

1. Turn the seam that needs repair inside out. With an adult supervising, use a warm iron to iron out the seam so that two edges of fabric meet, right sides facing.

2. With your chalk or pencil, mark an X at the stitching on both ends of the seam. Then, with your ruler and chalk or pencil, draw a straight line between the X's. Now you are ready to sew a running stitch along the seam.

3. You will sew with a double thread, so cut your thread not more than twice the length of your arm. If it is too long, it will tangle.

4. Thread your needle, then tie both ends in one knot.

5. Starting at one of the X's, pass the needle through the double fabric and gently pull until the knot catches on one side of it. Pass the needle back through the fabric close to where it came out. You have sewn one stitch. Try to make all your stitches about the same size by passing the needle through the fabric close to where it came out. Continue to guide your stitches along the line until you reach the other X. For a smooth line of stitches, pull the thread all the way through each time you pass the needle through the fabric. Be sure you do not pull the thread so tight that the fabric draws up into puckers. When your stitches reach the X on the opposite side, your seam is repaired.

6. Fasten your thread either by taking 3 tiny stitches clear through the cloth, one right on top of the other, or by pulling the needle through a loop, as shown in the picture. Cut the thread with scissors.

To fasten ends:

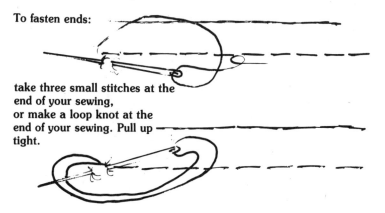

take three small stitches at the end of your sewing, or make a loop knot at the end of your sewing. Pull up tight.

7. Open the seam by ironing along the seam line on wrong side of fabric with a warm iron. Turn the garment right side out and see if you can tell where it was repaired.

IRON-ON PATCHES

Tears and worn spots on clothing are difficult to repair by sewing. An iron-on patch will cover a tear or worn spot and the area around it with a new-looking, smooth piece of fabric. These patches have a shiny adhesive on one side which sticks to fabric when heated with an iron. No sewing is necessary to apply an iron-on patch. Select a patch that matches the clothing to be repaired. Or you may want to create a colorful look by choosing a patch of contrasting color.

You will need —

1. iron-on patches;

2. scissors;

3. an iron;

4. an ironing board.

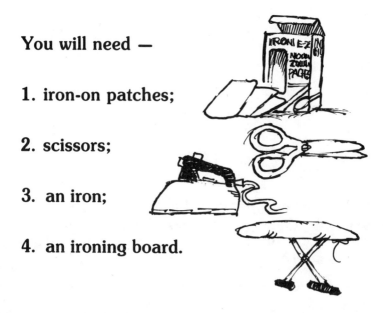

Heat the iron to **dry cotton**; this setting is HOT, so BE CAREFUL! We'll use jeans with torn knees as an example for this type of repair, but many kinds of clothing, especially those made of sturdy cotton, can be repaired with iron-on patches.

STEPS:

1. Lay the jeans on the ironing board with the torn knees face up.

2. Iron the tears smooth and heat the fabric to prepare it for the patch.

3. Cut the patch to fit over the tear and the area around it. Make the corners of the patch round instead of square.

4. Place the patch over the tear, shiny side down. (If the tear or worn spot is large, you will have to put a separate piece of fabric under the spot you are repairing so that your patch doesn't stick to the back of the pant leg.) Lay the iron on the patch and **slowly** move it around while you count **slowly** to 20. Move the iron around the edges to secure them.

5. Allow the patch to cool for 1 minute before handling. When the patch is cool, your pants are ready to wear.

TO REPAIR A HEM

When the stitching in a hem comes out, it can be repaired in several ways:

1. For a quick, temporary repair use masking tape to hold the unstitched hem in place.

2. Another quick and easy repair can be made with iron-on adhesive tape. This tape is a special material sold in strips at fabric stores.

   To use the tape for hem repair, you will need —

   - adhesive iron-on tape;
   - scissors;
   - an iron;
   - an ironing board.

With an adult supervising:

1. Cut a length of tape to fit along the unstitched portion of the hem.

2. Iron the unstitched hem even with the stitched part.

3. Place the tape along the top and inside the hem, laying it flat and even with the rest of the hem.

4. Slowly iron along the hem until the tape bonds the fabric together. When it cools, your hem is repaired.

You may also repair a hem by sewing it. You will need —

- thread to match the fabric of the hem;
- a small needle;
- scissors.

STEPS:

1. Cut a length of thread as long as your arm.

2. Thread the needle, knot the thread, and fasten under the hem.

3. Hold the fabric over your left forefinger, as in the picture.

4. Take a tiny stitch directly below the hem edge, picking up only one or two threads of the fabric. Bring the needle up through the hem edge about 1/2 inch away, and pull it through. Repeat (as in the picture), keeping the stitches fairly loose so they will not pucker.

5. Fasten your thread (see "To Repair a Seam") and cut the thread with scissors.

THE END of not taking care of your own clothes.